Craigen Castle Mystery

Rod Smith

Richmond READERS

Richmond READERS

Craigen Castle Mystery

Joan and Ed are taking a holiday because Joan has been ill. They visit Craigen Castle, a medieval building with an unusual design. When they turn to go home, they find that someone has locked the main door to the castle. They cannot get out. As night falls, the past begins to come alive. Strange and frightening things begin to happen .... What is the mystery of Craigen Castle?

....

Rod Smith is a writer and a teacher. He was born in Oxford, England, but now he lives in Paraguay with his wife and young son. When he is not working, Rod likes taking long walks in the country and playing the piano.

LEVEL 2

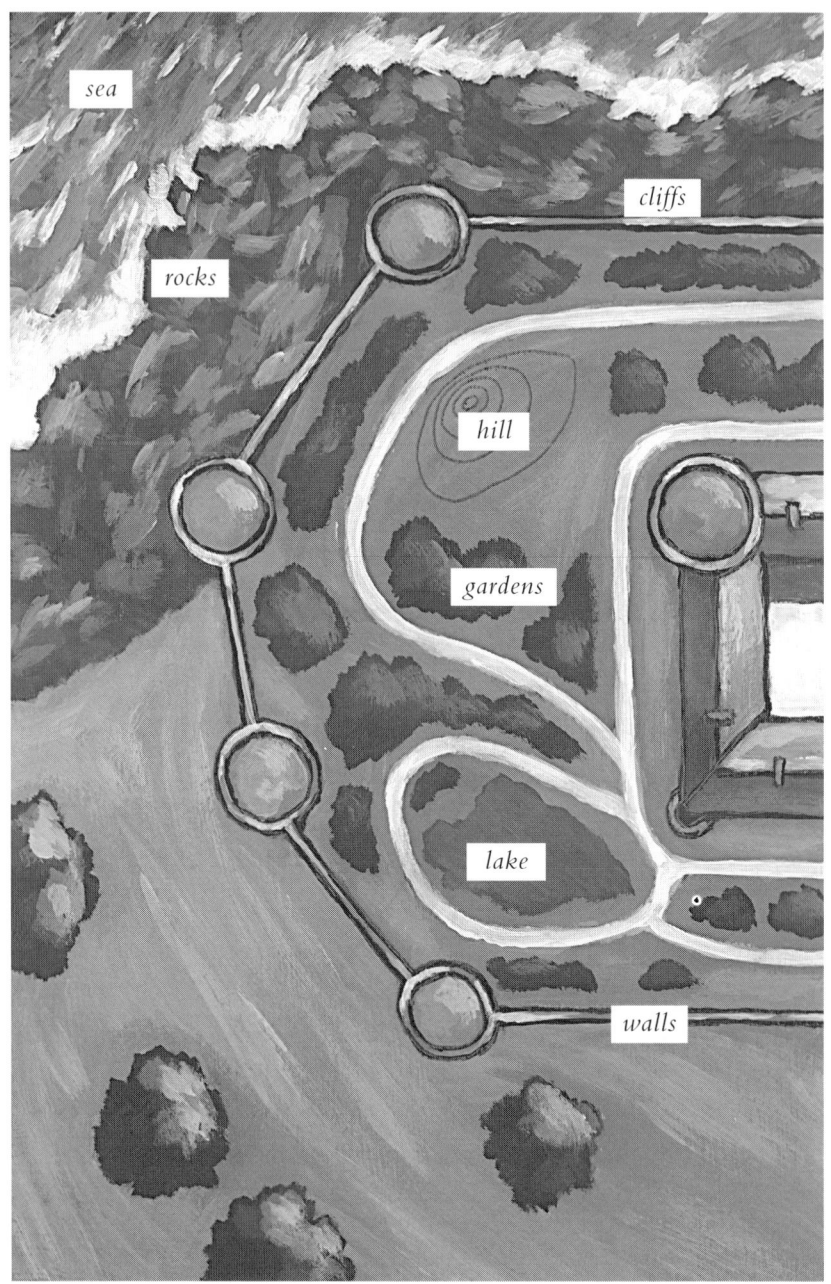

sea

cliffs

rocks

hill

gardens

lake

walls

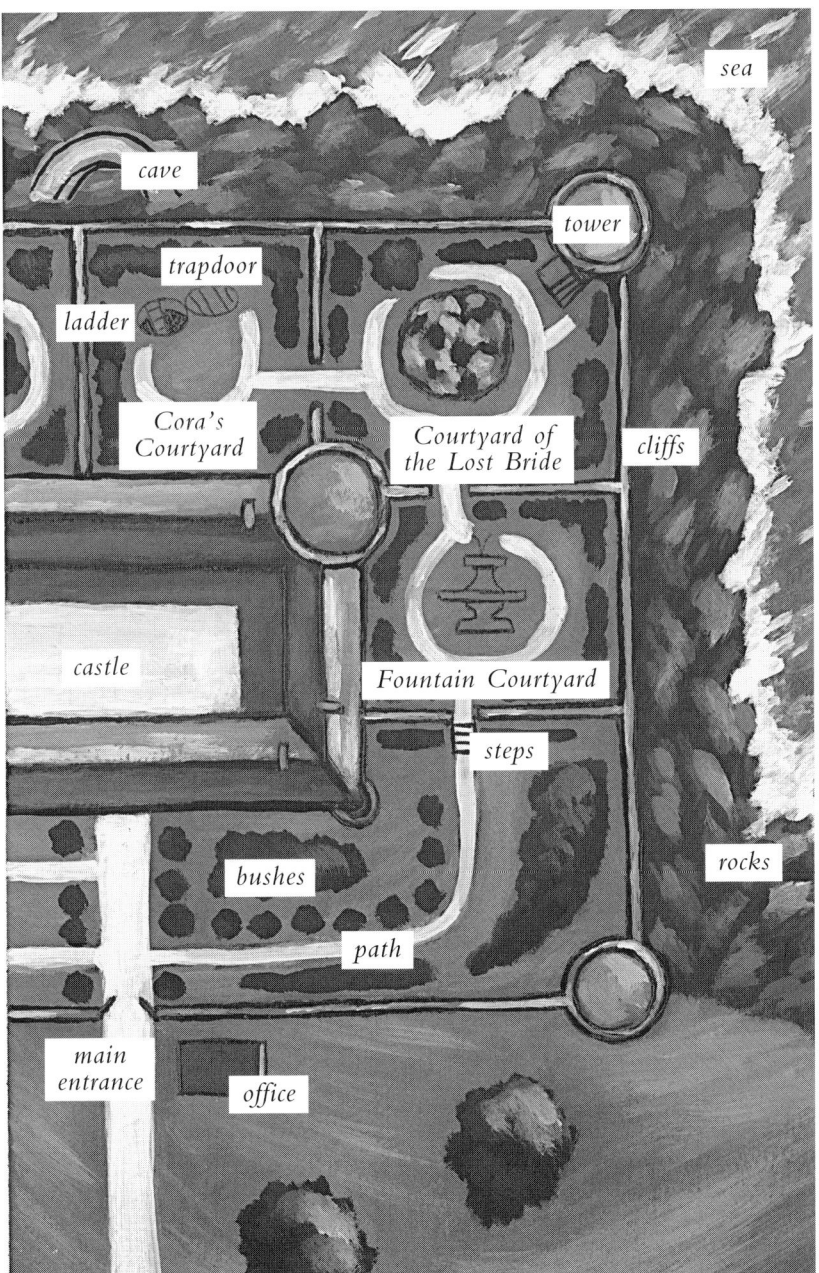

sea

cave

tower

trapdoor

ladder

Cora's
Courtyard

Courtyard of
the Lost Bride

cliffs

castle

Fountain Courtyard

steps

bushes

rocks

path

main
entrance

office

Author's note

This story happens on an island in north-west Scotland. It is not a real island, but there are many similar islands in the area. In winter the weather can be very cold, but the sea is relatively warm. This is because of the Gulf Stream, a warm ocean current which goes from the Gulf of Mexico, up the Atlantic coast of north America and north-eastwards towards Scotland. For this reason it is possible to grow some tropical plants on these Scottish islands. Many exotic plants grow in the courtyards* of Craigen Castle.

CHAPTER 1
Holiday in Onach

My wife and I are standing in the gardens of Craigen Castle. The castle is on an island in north-west Scotland. It is built on the edge of a cliff, high above the sea.

Opposite the island on the mainland is the village of Onach. A bridge joins the island to the mainland. My wife was born in Onach, but she doesn't really know the village very well. She left when she was young and hasn't been back there since.

Craigen Island

Onach

The island belongs to Lord William Douglas. It has belonged to the Douglas family for hundreds of years. Until recently, Craigen was the family home. But castles are expensive to maintain*, so now Lord Douglas only lives here in the summer. When he is here, Craigen Castle is open to visitors. July is the most popular month. In July the gardens are bright with flowers and full of people.

It's not July now and there are no visitors. It's December – a cold, dark month – and we are alone.

There's a book in my hand. It's called *Craigen: Castle and Grounds**.

'Where are we exactly?' my wife asks. She's nervous*. She speaks quickly and her voice sounds higher than normal. That's good. I wait a few seconds before opening the book. There's a map on the first page.

'Let *me* see.' She pulls the book from my hand and walks away.

'Relax, Joan.'

But Joan isn't listening. She stands at a distance, studying the map.

I close my eyes and try to imagine life without Joan. In a few hours I won't need to. I'll be alone again – forever. The thought makes me smile.

'Show me where we are.' I open my eyes. Joan is standing in front of me. She's holding the book. I take it from her and point to the word 'hill' in the top left corner of the map.

'We're a long way from the main entrance*,' she says, looking at her watch. 'Come on. It's four o'clock. We should go.'

I say nothing. Snow covers the distant high ground. I feel cold looking at it. I turn to look at the trees. It's getting dark now. But I can still see the lake, and far above it, a single bird flying over the old castle walls.

How calm everything is. How silent. And how sad that Joan doesn't seem to enjoy being here. She should. For this is what she needs – somewhere quiet where she can relax. It's because of her that we're here, you see. Because of her illness, that is.

■ ■ ■

It was Alan's idea to come here. Alan is an old friend. Now he is also our business partner. We have a small company in Glasgow. The company makes clothes. All three of us work there: Alan, Joan and I. My name is Edward, Edward Sutton. But everyone calls me Ed.

I am Joan's second husband. Her first husband, John Roag, was a rich man. He died ten years ago and left all his money to* Joan. After Joan and I were married, she used some of the money to start the company. For years it was very successful, but recently we lost one of our most important clients. We lost him because of Joan.

The client came into the office one day to talk about dates for his clothes order*. The meeting went well at first. Then Joan became angry for no reason.

I see a single bird far above the lake, flying toward the old castle walls.

She told the client that he was stupid. He left without saying anything more. The next day she phoned to say she was sorry. But it was too late. He wrote a letter cancelling all his orders.

After this incident, life in the office got worse. Joan began to imagine that everyone hated her. She became temperamental. One minute she was calm and rational; the next minute she was screaming* at everyone. At night she had terrible dreams and woke up crying.

I thought she was going mad*. I didn't want to work with her or live with her any more. But I needed her money.

Alan was very unhappy about Joan. The business was very important to him; it was his life. He didn't want her to destroy* it. Then Alan told me about his plan. I liked it. I said we should go ahead*.

So, one day last summer, Alan came here to Onach, alone. Early one morning he drove over to the island and went to the castle office, which is outside the main entrance. There were some keys on the wall. He waited until no one was looking and took the keys. Then he went to a nearby town, where copies were made. He returned the original keys before anyone saw that they had gone.

That was the first part of the plan.

Autumn came. Joan got worse. At the end of November, Alan said to her, 'You need a holiday. Let's all take a winter holiday together – in Onach, where you were born.' She agreed.

So now all three of us are here in Onach.

After lunch in the hotel today, Alan said he was tired. 'I want to stay in my room and read,' he said. 'You two go to the island. We can meet back here later.'

When Joan wasn't looking, he gave me one of the keys. It was all part of the plan.

■ ■ ■

'Come on, Ed. We shouldn't be here. Let's go.'

We begin to walk along the path towards the main entrance. I walk as slowly as I can. Joan walks beside me. I can tell that she feels nervous about the time.

I want her to think of something else, so I show her the book I'm holding.

'Have you read this?' I ask.

'No.'

'So you don't know the story of the three courtyards*?'

'The story of what?'

'The three courtyards. They're on the other side of the castle, in the corner nearest the sea.'

'No, I don't.' She sounds interested, but a little afraid.

'Then I'll tell you.'

I don't need the book. I know the story well.

Alan waited until no one was looking and took the keys.

———— CHAPTER **2** ————

The Story of the Three Courtyards

'Inside the walls of Craigen Castle there are three courtyards. They are all very beautiful – full of trees and exotic plants. But behind each one there is a tragic story.' Joan moves closer.

'The first one is called the Fountain Courtyard. It was here, in the year 1397, that the third Lord Douglas was killed by his enemies*. They tied him to one wall of the courtyard in front of the fountain. They didn't give him any food or water. He died very slowly. At night, when the moon is full, they say you can hear him crying out* for water.'

Joan's hand closes around my arm. It hurts, but I continue.

'The second courtyard is called the Courtyard of the Lost Bride*. Here, on the night his son was married, in October 1486, the sixth Lord Douglas gave a large party. During the party, towards midnight, he announced a game. He stood up, holding a large bag of money.

'"Ladies," he said. "Go and hide*. Those of you who are not found until after midnight will share this money!"

'The women ran away laughing. They were all found. All except one – his son's bride. They looked for her everywhere, but she was never found. Many years later, some men were working on the roof* of the tower*

They tied him to one wall of the courtyard in front of the fountain.

above the second courtyard. Under the roof they found an old metal chest. Inside was the skeleton of a young woman. Here was the "lost bride". After she had got inside the chest, the lock* had closed and she couldn't get out. They now say that on some nights, when all is calm, you can hear the sound of her trying to get out...'

'That's enough,' says Joan.

'The third courtyard is simply called Cora's Courtyard. This story is more recent.'

'Ed, stop, please. I'm afraid.'

'Thirty years ago, the Douglas family had a lot of servants*. The servants lived in the part of the castle which is above the third courtyard. The youngest was a girl of fifteen. Her name was Cora Hay. Cora had a friend, an older girl called Liz, who also worked in the castle. Cora and Liz both liked a man called Ian Jardine, who worked in the gardens. But it was Liz that Ian fell in love with. It wasn't long before they were married; and the following year Liz had a baby boy. Cora was very jealous*. Every day she became more jealous. Finally, two years later, she decided to leave the castle.

'The day before she was going to leave, there happened to be a big summer party in the village. Most of the people who worked in the castle went to the party. By early evening only four people were still in the castle – Liz, Ian, their little boy and Cora. Cora was in the third courtyard watering the plants. Ian came into the courtyard with his little boy. He told

Under the roof they found an old metal chest. Inside was the skeleton of a young woman.

Cora that they were going on to the party. He asked her to tell Liz where they were. But Cora, who now hated her old friend, saw her chance.'

'Ed, I don't want to hear this.'

'In the floor of the third courtyard, in one of the corners, there is a round trapdoor. The trapdoor is made of metal and is very heavy. Below it there is a ladder which goes down to a cave. Every few hours the sea comes in and the cave is completely filled with water. There is no way out.'

'This isn't funny, Ed. Stop, please.'

I pay no attention and continue.

'She waited until Ian and the child had gone. Then Cora opened the trapdoor. She found a hat that belonged to Liz's little boy and put it by the open trapdoor. Then she hid behind a tree and called out, "Mummy! Help!" Liz heard and came to the window above. She looked down and saw her little boy's hat by the open trapdoor. She screamed. Quietly, Cora left the courtyard.

'Later that night, young William Douglas - the present Lord Douglas - found Liz lying on the floor of the third courtyard. She was cold and wet. She had gone down the ladder into the cave. She had looked for her little boy until the water nearly filled the cave. Then, without hope, she had come back up the ladder. The next day she caught pneumonia. By the end of the month she was dead. Cora was never seen again.'

'Stop! Get me out of here - now!'

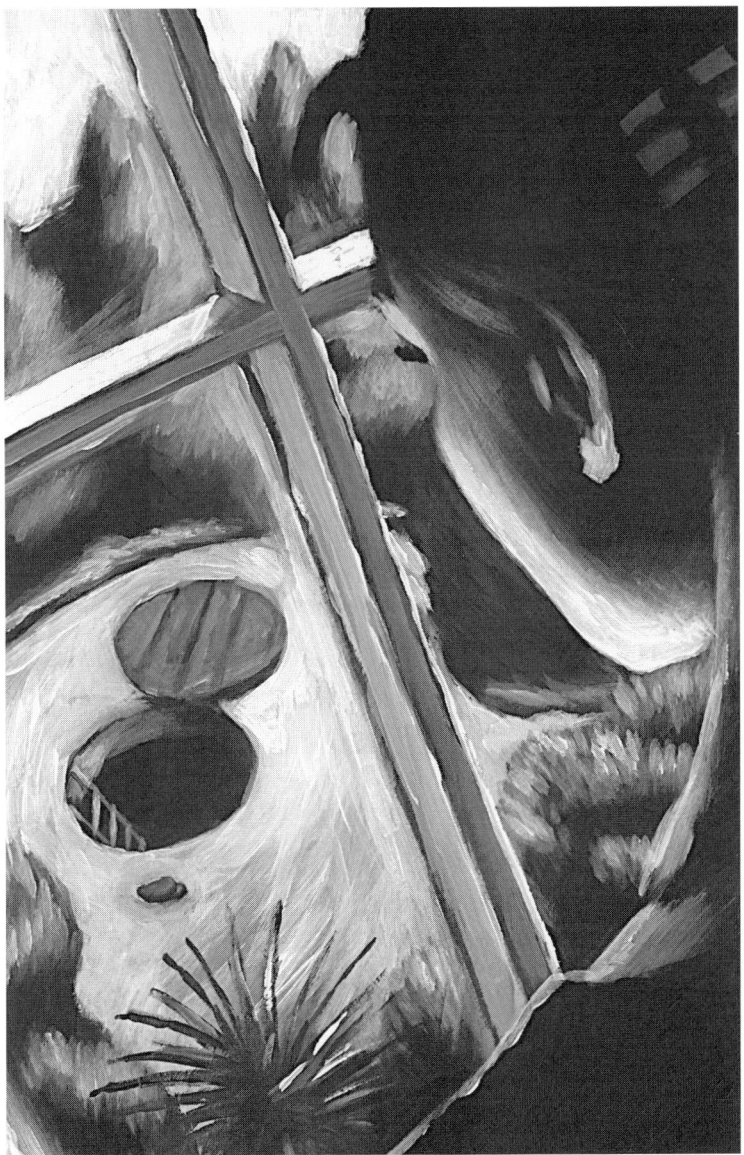

She looked down and saw her little boy's hat by the trapdoor.
She screamed.

'All right, all right,' I say, looking as calm as I can. 'There's no need to get angry. I thought you'd be interested, that's all.'

I begin to walk more quickly. It doesn't matter now. The main entrance door is locked and we are trapped* inside the castle. Of course, Joan doesn't know this. She doesn't know about the open door either, the one leading to the three courtyards.

It's all part of the plan.

——— CHAPTER **3** ———
Trapped!

We are standing by the main entrance. The ground is more open here and the north wind hits us hard. I cover my ears and watch Joan trying to open the door. It's a heavy door, very old, but very strong.

'I can't open it,' she says.

'Let me try.' I pull hard, but the door doesn't move.

'What's wrong?' asks Joan. 'Why won't it open?'

I turn towards her, looking serious. 'Because it's locked.'

'Locked?' Her face turns white. 'But how is that possible? It was open when we came here.'

'Yes, but–'

'You told me we were lucky to find the door open.' She is very angry now. '"Oh, look," you said, "we can go into the castle without paying,"' says Joan, imitating my voice. 'And now you tell me that the door is locked.'

'Well, clearly someone locked it while we were in the gardens.'

'What do you mean ... "someone"? Who? You told me that no one comes here in the winter.'

'Well, of course, there must be a gardener. The courtyards are full of trees and plants. Someone has to look after them, even in the winter. Lord Douglas probably pays someone from the village to work in the gardens when he's away. Maybe the gardener was working when we came here. The castle grounds are very big: we didn't see him and he didn't see us. The gardener has a key. That's why the door wasn't locked. When he left, he locked the door behind him. Why shouldn't he? He didn't know we were here.'

Joan turns towards the castle grounds. It's very cold. Ice lies like broken glass around the edges of the lake. She looks up. A circle of light – mysterious, unclear – touches the tops of the trees. There's going to be a full moon.

'We have to get out of here,' she says quietly.

I say nothing. I know getting out is impossible. The walls are at least thirty metres high, more in places. Joan is silent for a while, then she turns to me.

'There's no way out, is there?' she says.

'No, I don't think there is.'

She begins to cry.

Ice lies like broken glass around the edges of the lake. There's a full moon.

'What are we going to do? We'll die of cold.'

'No, we won't.' I am calm, relaxed. 'Listen. There's no way we can get inside the castle – all the doors and windows are locked. But I did see that the door to the three courtyards was open. We could go there and–'

'You mean those places you were telling me about? Where all those terrible things happened? You think we should spend the night there?'

'Yes. Why not? It'll be much warmer – we'll be out of the wind. There are lots of plants, too. Perhaps we can use them to make a bed.'

'I don't want to go in there.'

'Oh come on, Joan.' I hold her arm.

She pulls away from me.

'No. Leave me alone.'

'You want to stay here all night and die of cold?'

She doesn't answer.

'Joan.' My voice is softer, more serious. 'We'll have to – it's our only chance.' I hold her arm again. This time she doesn't pull away and we walk together along the path to the right of the castle.

■ ■ ■

At the end of the path there are six steps which go up to a door. The door stands above us, wide open, like a hungry black mouth.

Slowly, we go up the steps and into the three courtyards.

Chapter 4

The Fountain Courtyard

Night has come.

We're in the first courtyard, the one with the fountain. There is no water in the fountain. I'm sitting with my back against the castle wall. Joan is lying beside me. We've been here for six hours.

There are trees and bushes everywhere. Some have big leaves; others have small leaves. When we came into the courtyard, I broke some branches off and put them on the ground in a corner, under the far wall. Then Joan lay down and I used more branches to cover her body.

She's sleeping now. It's not a calm sleep. I can tell by the way her face moves that she's having a bad dream. I turn away. I dislike looking at the pain in Joan's face. For some reason it makes me angry.

How cold it is. Not as cold as by the main entrance, but still cold and getting colder. I ask myself how Joan can sleep. She'll soon wake up. By the early hours of the morning, even the branches won't be enough to keep her warm. Of course, that won't matter – it will be finished by then.

I look at my watch. Ten minutes to midnight. It's time to do what I have to do. I get up, quietly. I want to be sure Joan is still sleeping, so I stand above her - watching, waiting. She doesn't move. Good. I can leave. I follow the path to the left of the fountain and stop in front of the courtyard door. The door is closed now: I closed it after we came in. I take the key that Alan gave me and put it in the lock. Doing this gives me a strange feeling – a feeling that the walls around me are moving closer. I look up. Nothing but hard, flat rock, except for the windows of the castle, high above my head. Yes, it's just like Alan said. When the door to the three courtyards is locked, there's no way out ... I turn the key.

When I get back, Joan is still sleeping. I sit down beside her and look at my watch again. It's almost midnight – time to wake her up. I'm thinking of the best way of doing this when she turns, suddenly, and holds onto my arm.

'Ed?'

'What is it?'

'A dream, a terrible dream.'

'What about?'

'About what happened here. Oh Ed, don't...' She hides her face in my arm. It's difficult to hear what she's saying.

'I can't hear you, Joan.'

She looks up. 'Don't leave me. Just don't leave me, that's all.'

She sounds like a child who is afraid of the dark. I feel nothing for her: no love, no hate, nothing. When I answer, my voice is dead and low.

'I won't leave you. We must stay together.'

When the door to the three courtyards is locked, there is no way out ... I turn the key.

'Yes, but in my dream you weren't with me. I was afraid.'

Her voice is softer now, her eyes bigger. I know from this that she wants to feel closer to me. I smile. But Joan isn't stupid. She can see that the smile is false. Her eyes grow smaller, sadder. She knows she is alone with her feelings.

We sit with our backs to the wall, looking up at the night sky.

Clouds pass over the moon. The effect is strange. Everything around us turns from silver to black. The colours of the clouds change with the push and pull of the sea: sound and light synchronised. There are other sounds too: the call of an owl, the cry of the wind in the trees. But it is the music of the sea which holds our attention. There is something terrible in it. And then, as it pulls back from the coast, we hear something softer, the sound of water washing over rock. The rhythmic sound is like a drug.

Crash ... wash ... crash ... wash ... crash ... wash ...
Joan breathes* deeply. I feel her body moving to the sound of the sea. It makes me want to sleep.

Crash ... wash ... crash ... wat ... crash ... water ...
Joan stops breathing. I look at her. Her body is still, her mouth open.

'Are you all right?' I ask.

'That sound...'

'You mean the sea?'

Crash ... water! ... water! ...

There are other sounds too: the call of an owl...

'No.' She pulls my hand towards her. 'Listen. A voice. A horrible voice.'

'Control yourself, Joan.' But I, too, hear the voice. It's louder now and more regular. It comes from the direction of the fountain.

'My God! Can't you hear? It's like in the story.'

Water! … Water! … WATER! … WATER! …

The voice goes on getting louder. Suddenly, something long, thin and white appears from behind the leaves of a plant near the fountain. It is a man's hand.

Joan opens her mouth to speak, but no sound comes out. She can only watch, her eyes wide and bright with terror.

WATER! … Water! … Wat … crash … wash … crash

The voice gets softer. The hand falls. Then all is silent.

Joan closes her eyes and covers her ears.

I look at her in the way a doctor looks at someone who is ill.

'What's wrong with you, Joan?' I pull her hands away from her ears.

'The hand,' she says. 'Didn't you see the hand? All thin and white-'

'You're imagining things. It was probably just the branch of a tree, that's all.'

'But the voice...'

'There wasn't any voice. You saw and heard things which weren't there. It's just the effect of the light on

Suddenly, something long, thin and white appears from behind the leaves of a plant near the fountain.

the plants, and the sound of the sea. We'll be all right.'
I take her hand. 'We'll go to the next courtyard. It's
more open there. You won't feel so afraid.'

I stand up and help Joan to her feet. Slowly, we walk
towards the Courtyard of the Lost Bride.

Joan's dream is real now. And it's only just begun.

—————— CHAPTER **5** ——————

The Courtyard of the Lost Bride

We pass through an archway and go into the second
courtyard. In front of us is a structure, built of large
rocks. The rock structure is in the middle of the
courtyard. It looks like a small mountain. Plants grow
between the rocks and next to the walls. But there are
fewer plants here than in the Fountain Courtyard.
Behind the rock structure, in the far corner of the
courtyard, stands a high tower. It's a very strange
building, almost twice as high as the outside walls. It
seems too high. Steps go up to the entrance. There is
no door. At first I think there are no windows either.
But when we get closer I see that I was wrong. There
is one, only one. It's at the top of the tower and looks
over the sea.

We stop at the bottom of the steps.

'Do you think we should go inside?' asks Joan.

'I don't know. In the book it says there's a room at

Behind the rock structure, in the far corner of the courtyard, stands a high tower.

the top of the tower, where that window is. But there is no glass in the window – it's nothing more than a hole in the rock. It's much higher than where we were before. It'll be a lot colder.'

I remember how cold it is. I try not to think of the cold. But then I see something small and white fly through the air. Then another and another. Snow is falling.

'Oh God,' says Joan. 'What are we going to do?'

'Stay calm. I think the best place to spend the night is just inside the entrance to the tower. The walls of the tower will keep us dry, and warmer than out here.'

Joan stands completely still. She can't move. I put my arm around her and help her up the steps.

It's dark inside the entrance and the air smells of the sea. In front of us are more steps. They go up in a spiral to the top of the tower. I look up and remember the story of the lost bride. I imagine what happened all those years ago and my head fills with sounds: the sound of a young girl's feet running lightly up the steps above me, the sound of her laughing when she thinks of a good place to hide, the sound of the heavy chest closing over her, the sound of her cries for help. But no, I don't hear that. No one heard her cries for help.

And Joan? Is she thinking of these things? Maybe. She stands at the entrance, looking at the rock structure.

I thought it would be warmer here, but it isn't. It seems as cold inside the tower as it is outside.

Joan tries to control her body but the cold is too much.

This gives me the chance I've been looking for – a reason to leave. I stand next to her and speak softly.

'We need something to cover us. I'll have to go back to the first courtyard and get those branches we were using.'

Joan looks afraid.

'No, Ed. Don't leave me. Please.'

'Look. If we don't keep warm, we'll die. Is that what you want?'

She begins to cry.

'I don't know what I want any more. I don't know what's happening to me.'

I give her a serious look.

'Have you got your medicine with you?'

She stops crying. 'I think so.'

'Take it. You'll feel better.'

'Why are you always saying that? "Take the medicine. You'll feel better."' Again she imitates me. 'You think I'm mad, Ed, don't you? Maybe I am. Oh God. Help me.' She starts crying again.

I want to leave as quickly as possible. I hate the sound of her crying.

'Look, I'd better go now. I won't be long.'

She holds onto my arm.

'No. I'm coming with you.'

I don't know what to do. This isn't what I want, but I know that Joan won't stay here alone. I'll have to

This isn't what I want, but I know that Joan won't stay here alone.

take her with me.

We walk back down the steps and across the second courtyard. We go through the archway for the second time. Joan stops and looks up at the fountain. She doesn't want to go any farther. It's strange, but neither do I.

We stand together, neither of us moving.

All is quiet. Or is it? I listen hard. And then I hear something. It's the sound of music - medieval music - playing softly in the distance. The music gets louder. It comes from behind Joan. She turns and looks back towards the rock structure. There is light coming from inside the structure, light which burns like fire through the falling snow. This is my chance, my chance to hide. When Joan sees that she is alone, she'll be more afraid. And then? I smile to myself and begin to move away, as quietly as I can. There is a large bush next to one of the walls of the castle building. I hide myself behind it and look through the leaves. From my hiding place I can see into the second courtyard. And of course I can see Joan, standing in the archway. But she can't see me.

I look at the strange light. I feel excited. I know what's going to happen. Joan doesn't. She doesn't even know that I'm not there - all her attention is held by the bright light coming from the rocks. I watch for what seems like a long time. And then, from a space between two of the rocks, I see something small and round come out. It grows larger. Now I can see what it is. It is the back of a woman's head, the head of a bride, dressed in white. Slowly, the head turns.

It is the head of a bride, dressed in white.

There is no face, just a white skull*, whose mouth opens in a long, silent scream.

Joan moves backwards. She doesn't see that I'm not there. She sees only the terrible skull. But she calls my name and puts her hand out to touch me. There is nothing there.

She turns.

'Ed? ... For God's sake, Ed. Where are you?'

'This way, Joan.' I put my hand over my mouth so that my voice sounds far away.

She can't tell where I am. The music gets louder and the light gets brighter. She runs in the wrong direction and falls over a low branch. She gets up and runs to the door of the first courtyard – the door that I locked. When she can't open it, she hits it with her hands. I hear the sound of her breathing and her cries for help. Suddenly, the music stops and the light dies. I look back. There is no skull now. Once again, all is quiet and dark.

Joan lays her head against the courtyard door.

'Ed...?'

Her voice is soft, almost kind. I can imagine what she's thinking. She doesn't know that *I* locked the door. She's thinking the locked door is just one more of the terrible things which are happening to her, like the hand and the skull. She's thinking that what is happening isn't real, that it's all inside her head.

She turns. The fountain stands above her. I see the terror in her face, the look in her eyes that shows how

She drinks from the bottle and puts it back in her pocket.

much she wants to get away. But which way can she go? There is only one possible way. And that is through the third courtyard. Does she think that's where I've gone? I think so, from the way she talks. She tries to sound calm and imagines I can hear every word.

'You went the other way, Ed, didn't you? You went to find a way out. I made a mistake. I'm sorry. But I know where you are now, my love. I'm coming.'

She walks towards the second courtyard. There is a mad smile on her face, a look of hope in her eyes, stupid, false hope.

She stops at the archway and pulls something out of her pocket. It's a bottle of medicine. She drinks from the bottle and puts it back in her pocket. Then, after a while, she begins to go across the second courtyard. On the far side there is another archway – the entrance to the third courtyard. She walks towards it with her head up, like someone not wanting to see the things around them. She goes inside.

Cora Hay is waiting.

CHAPTER **6**
Cora's Courtyard

I wait a few seconds and then follow. I move quickly, but quietly, staying close to the castle walls. I stop beside the second archway, and listen. I hear Joan's voice calling my name. When it sounds far enough away, I go inside.

I see immediately that the third courtyard, like the first, is full of bushes. But here there are trees, too. Their leaves hide the sky. No snow gets through here. Everything is very dark.

Joan is standing under one of the trees, looking up. She has her back to me. Is she thinking that she can get onto the outside walls from the tree? That won't help her. There is only the cold, dark sea on the other side, waiting far below.

She goes into a dark corner. I can't see her now, but her mad voice goes on.

'I did what you said, Ed. I took the medicine. I feel much better now. I understand if you don't want to speak to me. But you're here, aren't you? You've found a way out. You're going to save us.'

Does she really think I'm up in that tree?

'Wait for me, Ed. I'm coming.'

I hear her trying to pull herself up by one of the branches. I hear the branch break. I hear a crash, followed by something soft and heavy falling to the ground. For a few moments all is quiet. Then Joan begins to cry.

I could kill her now. I don't want to. I want the plan to work. But I can't be sure that it will. And now would be a good time to kill her. Now, while she's lying at the bottom of the tree, all hope gone. I could walk up behind her, quietly, put my hands around her...

A sudden noise stops me. A door is being opened, a metal door. Joan stops crying. I feel a cold wind moving the leaves and branches around me. It carries with it the sound of the sea. It carries another sound, too – the sound of a small child calling out.

Mummy … Mummy … Help me!

Joan starts to cry again. But no, that's not Joan – it's another woman. Her cries are so sad that I almost feel like helping her.

And then someone laughs. The laugh is dry and unkind. The child's voice sounds far, far away. Now it's gone. The woman stops crying. Joan stands up. Something moves in the bushes in front of her. She watches and listens, her body as still as a rock. I hear the sound of someone pulling back leaves and branches, of feet, getting closer. And then I see a face, a young girl's face – the face of Cora Hay.

She has long black hair and her face is the colour of the moon, even her thin mouth. It is a face without expression, and yet it's the most evil face I have ever seen. Everything about it is dead. Except for the eyes which are burning with cold, green fire.

Joan screams – a long, hopeless scream that cuts through the air like a knife. I move back under the

Joan doesn't scream any more, but falls, silently, like the snow.

cover of the bushes and watch her. She runs from the third courtyard back to the tower, and up the steps. I hear the sound of her feet. The higher she goes, the softer the sound gets. Then there is nothing.

I look up. Joan is at the window at the top of the tower. Below her the sea is waiting. She moves forward. She doesn't scream any more, but falls, silently, like the snow.

It is finished. Joan is dead.

—— CHAPTER 7 ——
Through the Trapdoor

I stand below the tower for several minutes. It's colder than ever, but I don't feel the cold any more. I feel happy. I am alone again, and free – free of Joan, free of her illness, free to do what I want. And now I *can* do what I want, because the money that was hers is now mine. I'm a rich man.

I look around me. The snow is falling more heavily now. Everything is white and clean. The symbol of a new life - my new life alone.

I turn and go back into Cora's Courtyard. I walk over to the far corner nearest the sea, to the trapdoor in the floor which stands open. I look down into the deep hole in the rock. I look through the trapdoor at the cave far below and see the long ladder. The ladder goes down to the cave. I see a light at the bottom on a floor of wet, green rock.

I begin going down the ladder. It moves around a little because it's made of rope. But I don't care – I'm too excited.

Alan is standing at the bottom, waiting for me. He is a tall, thin man with dark eyes. On the ground beside him are the things he used to deceive* Joan: a cassette player, two latex masks, a torch*, a long white dress, false long black hair and a lamp with coloured glass. The lamp is burning. Alan's shadow dances on the walls of the cave. He doesn't speak, but there is a question in his eyes.

I answer it.

'Well done, Alan. The plan worked. She's dead.'

We smile. He pulls a small bottle of whisky from his pocket.

'Drink?' he asks.

'Why not?'

We drink from the bottle. Alan drinks a lot. He seems nervous. He feels bad about what we've done. That feeling will go. It will go when I pay him. He finishes the whisky.

'Let's get out of here,' he says.

I feel something cold at my feet and look down. Sea water, dark and wet, touches my shoes and washes in to the back of the cave.

'The sooner the better,' I say.

Alan throws the empty whisky bottle away.

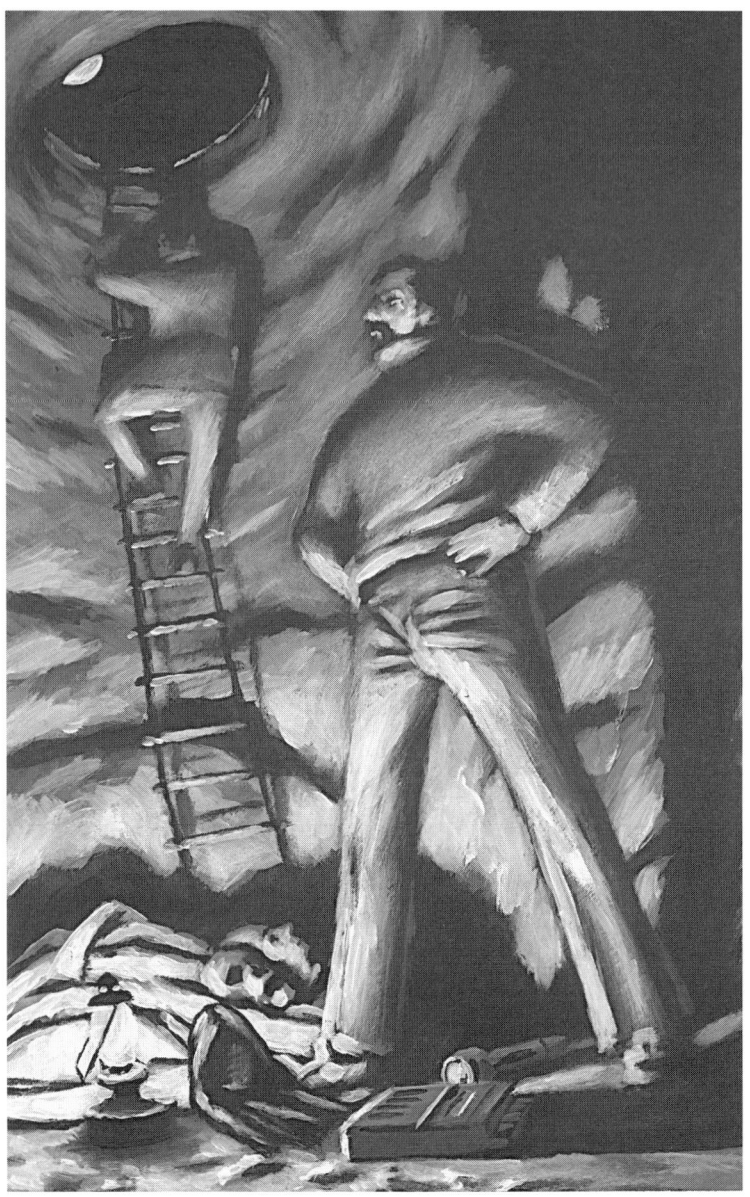

Alan's shadow dances on the walls of the cave.

'Ow,' he cries, holding his arm.

'What's wrong?'

'I hurt my arm coming down the ladder. I forgot about it. Now it hurts even more.'

'Can you get up the ladder?'

'I think so.' He picks up the lamp. 'I can take this, but do you mind carrying the rest of the things up for me? You can put everything in the dress and use it as a bag.'

'No problem.'

Alan moves to the ladder, then turns.

'You'd better give me the key to the courtyard. I'll go and open the door while you're bringing the things up. I'll leave the lamp at the top of the hole so you can see your way up.'

'OK.' I give him the key and start putting everything inside the dress.

It probably takes me no more than a minute to do this, but it seems a lot longer. When everything's ready, I go to the ladder. I look up. Alan is at the top of the hole now. I see his feet for a second, then nothing. I begin to go up.

'Give me the key.'

I know that voice. It isn't Alan's.

Alan is holding the key. I see his hand move across the top of the hole. Another hand meets it and takes the key.

My blood turns to ice.

Seconds later, a face looks down at me. It's a face I thought I would never see again.

I see Alan's hand move across the top of the hole. Another hand meets it and takes the key.

It is Joan. She smiles.

'Hello, Ed.' There is a knife in her hand. She gives it to Alan. He begins to cut the rope at the top of the ladder.

My mouth opens and closes stupidly.

'But I ... I saw ... I ...' No more words come out.

'You saw me die, Ed? Is that what you were going to say?' I can't answer. I feel little bits of rope falling on my face.

'But that wasn't me you saw, Ed,' she goes on. 'It was a dummy* dressed in the same clothes as me. While you were hiding in the first courtyard, Alan was putting the dummy in the tower. That's why I stopped to drink the medicine. To give him time.'

'But ... the plan? I don't understand. I...'

'Oh, Ed. You don't still think all this was Alan's idea, do you? Of course not. It was mine. You were the one being deceived, not me. You see, Alan and I want to get married. We also want to have the company for ourselves. Because I can't divorce you, Ed. If I do, you get half my money and half the company. That's no good. I want all of it, Ed. All of everything. I've always been like that. Funny, isn't it? I mean, funny that you thought I was so different - sad, little Joan. You're really not a very intelligent man, are you Ed?'

The ladder breaks on one side. I hold on by a single rope. It's difficult to breathe and there's a noise in my head - the noise my heart is making.

Joan puts her hand on the knife.

'Wait,' she says. Alan stops cutting. She stops smiling. Her face is hard and cold now.

'Think of this, Ed. In a few hours' time the cave will be full of sea water. You will either drown* or die of cold. No one will save you. Don't you remember what you told me? "No one comes here in the winter." Those were your exact words.' She turns to Alan. 'Cut the rope and lock him in. I'll go and open the door.'

'Joan. Please don't do it.'

She looks down at me and says the last two words I will ever hear her say.

'Goodbye, Ed.'

'Joan. Wait.' But it's too late. She's gone.

Alan keeps cutting. I cry for him to stop. But his face is as cold as the mask of Cora Hay.

Seconds later, the rope breaks and I fall to the ground. I feel a pain in my leg and look up. I can see very little, but I hear a great crash. The crash of heavy metal on rock.

Then everything goes black.

Lord William Douglas finished reading and passed the last of the papers over to Inspector McCabe.

The Inspector pushed them back into the empty whisky bottle.

'So, there you are,' he said, 'while Edward Sutton was waiting to die, he wrote down his story on the inside pages of this book.'

Lord Douglas looked down at the book cover lying on his desk. It was still wet, all the inside pages were gone and the words on the front, *Craigen: Castle and Grounds*, were difficult to read.

The Inspector went on, 'He wrote in the empty spaces around the edges of each page. Difficult. We think the only light he had came from a small torch we found in the pocket of his jacket.'

Lord Douglas sat down. He felt tired. The last eight hours were like a bad dream. He remembered the phone call from the police, the long car journey from Edinburgh to Onach along roads covered in snow. He remembered arriving at the castle and the crowd of village people standing outside the main entrance.

He remembered Inspector McCabe's first words.

'Good afternoon, Lord Douglas. Thank you for getting here so quickly. You've probably heard what's happened. Before I tell you exactly what we know, I'd

Lord Douglas remembered arriving at the castle that morning.

like you to read these papers. A young boy found them on Onach beach at around six thirty this morning. They were in an empty whisky bottle. They were written by a man called Edward Sutton. We found his body inside the cave below Craigen Castle. We can't be sure exactly when he died, but we think it was about a week ago.'

It had taken forty minutes for Lord Douglas to read Sutton's tragic story. It was the story of a very bad man, and not a very intelligent one. But William Douglas had a kind heart. He felt sorry that anyone should die in the way Edward Sutton had.

The Inspector walked around the desk and stood at the window. When he spoke, his voice was deep and serious.

'We found the other one over there.'

Lord Douglas turned, quickly.

'What?' he said. 'I don't understand.'

'The other one. Didn't you know? We found a second body – at the bottom of that tower.'

Lord Douglas went to join the Inspector at the window. They looked across at the tower in the second courtyard.

'In there? My God. But who? How...?'

'It was the body of Alan Cotmore. He died of cold. It seems clear to us that while he was cutting the rope, Joan Sutton left the courtyards and locked him inside. He couldn't get out. We don't think it took him long to die. He was wearing very thin things so that it was easier for him to change clothes quickly. Good for the plan, but not for the cold.'

'But why should Joan Sutton want to kill him? I thought...?'

'That they were in love?' the Inspector smiled sadly. 'No. Cotmore was, maybe, but she wasn't. She just used him to kill her husband. When the job was done, she didn't need him any more.'

'I see. And ... have you caught her?'

'No,' said the Inspector, moving his head slowly from side to side. 'And she's probably left the country by now, taking all her money with her.' He went on to explain. 'You see, when we started looking for her, we used the wrong name.'

'You mean Sutton?'

'Not exactly. We already knew that she had another name. She was married before, you see. Her first husband was a man called John Roag. He died mysteriously, soon after they were married. After his death Joan kept his name. So Edward Sutton always knew her as Joan Roag. But that wasn't her real name, the name she was born with. We found out what that was from papers in her office. It's a name I think you've heard before, Lord Douglas.'

'Oh?'

'Yes. It's Hay – Cora Joan Hay. She used to work here, I believe.'

Lord Douglas couldn't answer. A picture of a desperate woman came into his mind. A woman who

Outside, the winter snow continued to fall.

thought her child was dead, lying cold and wet beside a trapdoor.

He turned away and looked out of the window.

■ ■ ■

Outside, the winter snow continued to fall. It covered everything that had been the Douglas family home for so many years: walls, gardens, roofs, towers. It also covered the three courtyards. With their snow covering they looked different - uninteresting, almost - like the corner of a quiet street in the great white city that was now Craigen Castle.

He wished they could stay that way - forever.

EXERCISES

A Comprehension

Chapter 1 Holiday in Onach
1 Why doesn't Lord William Douglas live in the castle?
2 When is the castle busy?
3 When is it quiet?
4 Why is Joan nervous?
5 What kind of company do Ed and Joan have?
6 Who started the company?
7 Why doesn't Ed want to live with Joan any more?
8 How can Ed get Joan's money without living with her?

Chapter 2 The Story of the Three Courtyards
1 What happened in the first courtyard in the year 1397?
2 Where did the Lost Bride die?
3 Why was Cora jealous of Liz?
4 Where did William Douglas find Liz when he returned from the party?
5 What happened to Cora Hay?
6 How does Ed know that the main entrance is locked?

Chapter 3 Trapped!
1 Ed and Joan paid to go into the castle. True or false?
2 The gardener locked the main entrance after he left. True or false?
3 There is a full moon. True or false?
4 Joan thinks they will die from cold. True or false?
5 Ed and Joan saw that the door to the three courtyards was open. True or false?
6 Ed doesn't want to go into the three courtyards. True or false?

Chapter 4 The Fountain Courtyard
1 Who said, 'A dream, a terrible dream.'?
2 Who said, 'Water! ... water! ...?
3 Who said, 'It's like in the story.'?

4 Who said, 'Didn't you see the hand?'?
5 Who said, 'It was probably just the branch of a tree...'?
6 Who said, 'It's more open there. You won't feel so afraid.'?

Chapter 5 The Courtyard of the Lost Bride
1 Why does Ed describe the tower in the second courtyard as 'strange'?
2 Why does Joan say, 'Oh God. What are we going to do?'?
3 Where does the light come from?
4 What happens inside the rock structure?

Chapter 6 Cora's Courtyard
1 How does Joan try to escape from the third courtyard?
2 What does Joan do when she sees the face of Cora Hay?

Chapter 7 Through the Trapdoor
1 Why does Ed think that Alan is nervous?
2 Why does Ed want to leave the cave quickly?
3 Why does Alan say there is something wrong with his arm?
4 When does Ed first know that Joan is not dead?
5 Why did Alan and Joan deceive Ed?
6 Where does Joan go while Alan cuts the rope and locks the door to the cave?

Epilogue
1 How could Ed see to write down the story?
2 What did he do after he wrote it?
3 Why was Lord Douglas tired?
4 Why did Joan leave Alan to die?
5 What do you think really happened to Joan's first husband, John Roag?
6 Why didn't Ed know what Joan's real name was?

B Working with Language

I Find information in the story to complete these sentences.

a Ed wants to kill Joan because...
b After they left the tower, Ed and Joan went...
c Joan didn't want to go into the three courtyards because...
d When Joan fell from the tower, Ed thought...
e Ed thought that Alan was his friend, but...
f Joan asked Alan for the key to the three courtyards because...

2 These sentences describe what happens in Chapter 5. Put them in the right order.

a Joan begins to cry.
b Ed hides behind one of the plants.
c Ed and Joan see a large rock structure which looks like a small mountain.
d Snow begins to fall.
e Joan tries to leave the three courtyards, but the door is locked.
f Ed and Joan go into the tower.

C Activities

I Write a short newspaper report about how Ed and Alan died. Either write your own headline or use one of these:

THE RETURN OF CORA HAY

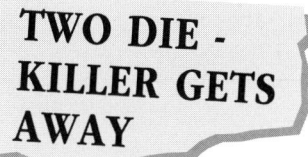

TWO DIE - KILLER GETS AWAY

2 Imagine Joan's plan to kill Ed and Alan. You are Joan. Either draw a diagram or write a paragraph describing your plan.

3 Joan says that Ed is 'not a very intelligent man'. Why does she say this? How could Ed have been more clever?

GLOSSARY

breathe *(v)* to take air into your body through your nose or mouth

bride *(n)* a woman who is getting married

courtyard *(n)* a room with four walls open to the sky

cry out *(v)* to call out loudly because you are unhappy in some way

deceive *(v)* to make someone believe something which is not true

destroy *(v)* to ruin

drown *(v)* to die by taking water into your body

dummy *(n)* used to show new clothes in a shop window

enemy *(n)* a person who hates you or wants to hurt you; *plural* **enemies**

entrance *(n)* a way into a building

go ahead *(v)* to begin to do something which you have agreed before, e.g. a plan

grounds *(n)* an area of private land, usually large, around a building

hide *(v)* to put yourself in a place where you cannot be seen or found easily

jealous *(adj)* feeling angry towards another person because they have what you want

leave something to someone *(v)* If John *leaves* some money *to* Jack, when John dies, Jack will get the money

lock *(n)* a lock is opened and closed with a key; *(v)* secure a door with a key

maintain *(v)* to keep something in good condition

mad *(adj)* lunatic/demented

nervous *(adj)* be afraid and not relaxed

order *(n)* *(business)* a request for products

roof *(n)* the roof covers the top of a building and protects the interior from the weather

scream *(v)* to use your voice very loudly, either because you are afraid or angry

servant *(n)* someone who is paid to do domestic work in another person's house

skull *(n)* hard part of the head (bones)

torch *(n)* a pocket light powered by batteries

tower *(n)* a tall, thin building, often circular

trapped *(adj)* be unable to get out of a difficult situation

Richmond

58 St Aldates
Oxford
OXI IST
United Kingdom

Publishing Director: Sarah Thorpe
Managing Editor: Tanya Whatling
Editor: Jane Holt

Cover Illustration: Manuel Uhía
Illustrations: Mark Oldroyd
Recording: Maria Jeanette Christiansen, Mauri Corretjé

Printed in Spain
ISBN: 978-84-668-1590-1

© Richmond / Santillana Educación S.L., 2012